An Introduction to

European Swords

COVER ILLUSTRATION: *Left* Small-sword, the steel hilt and scabbard
mounts chiselled in low relief and gilt, the blade inscribed THOMAS DE
AYALLA, German, about 1750.
The fine workmanship on this hilt suggests it may be the work of a
medallist.
Blade l. 67.5 cm. Hilt l. 13.2 cm.
M.48–1967.

Centre Small-sword, the hilt of gilt bronze, the grip of painted
enamel.
German, about 1750.
Blade l. 74.3 cm. Hilt l. 14.4 cm.
142–1889.

Right Small-sword, the hilt of chiselled and gilt steel.
Russian (Tula), about 1755.
Blade l. 77.5 cm. Hilt l. 13.6 cm.
1731–1888.

An Introduction to

European Swords

Anthony North

Research Assistant, Department of Metalwork
Victoria & Albert Museum

LONDON: HER MAJESTY'S STATIONERY OFFICE

Edited by Anthony Burton
Designed by Andrew Shoolbred
to a series design by Humphrey Stone
Produced by Pitman Books Ltd, London.

ISBN 0 11 290378 9
Dd 696417 C25

The Medieval Sword

The sword has always occupied a high position in the hierarchy of weapons. Its symbolic importance is reflected in its role in coronations, and the sword often accompanied a warrior to his grave.

The knightly sword of the Middle Ages probably derived from the earliest iron swords used by the Celtic peoples, and its immediate ancestors are the broad straight swords of the Vikings. It consisted of a long broad blade balanced by a substantial pommel; the guard to protect the hand, or 'quillon', was in the form of a short bar at right angles to the blade, with a grip of wood bound with leather or cord. The blade was usually double-edged and straight. Swords with only one edge or with broad cleaver-like blades have survived from the Middle Ages but they are comparatively rare.

Although at first the medieval sword was designed as a cutting weapon, during the 13th century the point came to be used in preference to the edge, probably as a result of the development of plate armour. In consequence, by the second quarter of the 14th century, blades were made much narrower with long points, of diamond or hexagonal section. By the middle of the 13th century the grip had also been extended so that the sword could now be held with both hands. The cross-guard, which before had been either straight or only slightly curved, also changed: by 1450 it often curved sharply towards the blade. The earlier wheel-shaped pommel was now supplanted by pommels of triangular, conical or oval section. By the 15th century in certain areas national characteristics in the design of hilts were beginning to emerge; hilts from the Germanic countries for example had quillons curving in a horizontal S-shape. In Italy, in the latter part of the 15th century, a sword with a short but very wide blade was fashionable.

Manuscript illuminations sometimes depict warriors holding swords with the forefinger curled around the base of the blade. From the early 15th century an extra guard is often found, in the form of an open ring attached to the top of the quillon,

5

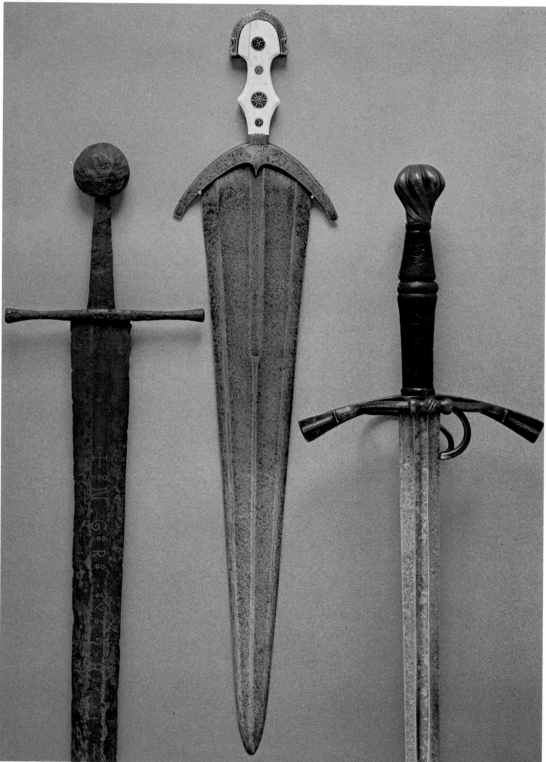

1
Sword, found in Whittlesea
Mere, Huntingdonshire.
English, about 1300, the blade
inlaid with laton letters
Blade l. 88 cm. Hilt l. 16.3 cm.
Private Collection.

2
Sword (*cinquedea*), the blade
with traces of etching, the hilt
of ivory mounted in gilt
bronze.
Italian, about 1500.
Blade l. 53 cm. Hilt l. 15.3 cm.
478–1901.

3
Hand and a half sword, the hilt
of blued and chiselled steel.
German, about 1500.
Blade l. 98 cm. Hilt l. 21 cm.
M.602–1927.

4
Pommel, quillons and
by-knife, gilt iron encrusted
with silver.
English, about 1610.
On the knife is the mark of the
Cutlers Company of London,
and that of John Bushnell, the
maker. These mounts are from
a sword long in the possession
of the Kimberley family, and
were probably made by Robert
South, the Royal Cutler to
James I and Charles I.
D. of pommel 5.3 cm.
L. of quillons 17.4 cm.
L. of knife 20.4 cm.
M.28 & a–1975.

acting as a protection for the forefinger. Perhaps for the sake of
symmetry, or more probably so that the sword could be used
with either edge, from about 1450 onwards a similar open ring
guard was added to the other quillon. By the end of the 15th
century the two ring guards were linked by an additional ring-
guard set horizontally; and an extra guard curving from the base
of the quillons to the pommel was provided to protect the
knuckles. However there is no regular line of development in
the design of sword hilts. It should not be thought, for example,
that the simple cross-hilt was entirely abandoned; it remained
in use for executions and certain ceremonial purposes until the
19th century.

The Rapier
For several reasons the sword underwent a variety of changes
in the 16th century. First, public combat in the lists was replaced
by duelling in private; this led directly to the development of
fencing which in turn affected the design of swords. Secondly,
the tendency throughout the 15th century was for swords to be
made lighter. As they had become an essential adjunct of civilian
dress, they were consequently much more decorative. Thus the
invention of the rapier – the civilian sword *par excellence* worn
from the 1530s to the 18th century. The rapier was probably
first developed in Spain, for early literary references describe
the rapier as 'a Spanish sword'. The word 'rapier' probably
derives from the Spanish term *espada ropera* – meaning a costume
sword. The earliest rapiers of about 1530 had long two-edged

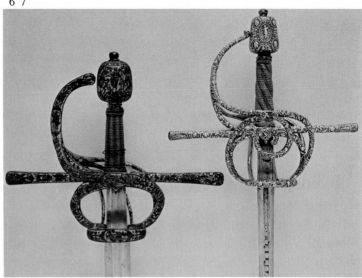

5
Portrait of Robert Devereux, 2nd Earl of Essex (1566–1601). School of Gheeraerts, about 1600.
The picture shows the Earl wearing a swept-hilt rapier, together with a dagger, both decorated *en suite* suspended from an embroidered sword belt.
National Maritime Museum.

6
Rapier, the steel hilt chiselled, blued and gilt with designs after Etienne Delaune. By Daniel or Emanuel Sadeler of Munich, the blade inscribed with the Running Wolf mark. German (Bavaria) about 1600.
Blade l. 106.5 cm. Hilt l. 15.5 cm.
M.52–1947.

7
Rapier, the steel hilt gilt and encrusted with silver.
Italian ? about 1600.
The blade is inscribed ME FECIT SOLGN (*sic*) indicating it was made at Solingen.
Blade l. 104 cm. Hilt l. 19.1 cm.
M.53–1947.

blades which could be used for cutting and thrusting, short grips, and a guard formed of interlinked rings and bars. The narrow long blades probably developed as a result of the influence of the Italian fencing schools with their emphasis on using the point of the sword; rapiers have survived in original condition with blades as long as 1.5 metres specially designed for fencing. The length of the rapiers carried by civilians seems to have been the subject of contemporary controversy. John Stow (c. 1525–1605) wrote of certain 'grave citizens' positioned by Royal decree at every gate to the City of London whose duty it was 'to break the Rapier's poynts of all passengers that exceeded a yeard in length of their Rapier' (*sic*).

When a system of fencing with both rapier and dagger was introduced in the first half of the 16th century, the hilts of these two weapons were usually decorated *en suite*. The rapier scabbard was suspended from the belt in a form of sling, sometimes lavishly embroidered and decorated, the dagger being fitted close to the belt. The rapier hilt became more complex as extra bars were added to protect the hand. In about 1560–70 the swept-hilt first appeared: this was made up of interlinked bars and rings in front of and behind the guard, sweeping in an elegant curve from the rear of the hilt to the knuckle-guard. The network of bars did not afford much protection from the point of a sword even when used with a glove reinforced with plates. Certain German swords with stiff triangular-sectioned blades known in England as 'tucks', from the French *estoc*, were fitted from about 1570 with a pierced plate as a protection against the point. By the end of the 16th century the gaps between the guards at the back and the ring-guard at the front

8

9 10

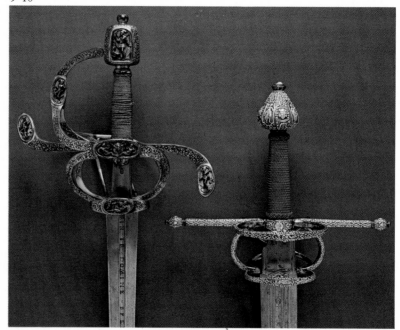

11 12

8
Rapier, the hilt of steel.
German, about 1550, the blade
inscribed SEBASTIAN
HERNANEZ.
Blade l. 86.4 cm. Hilt l. 22.5
cm.
M.92–1930.

9
Rapier, the steel hilt chiselled,
gilt and damascened in gold
and silver, the blade inscribed
IVAN MARTINEZ IN TOLLET and
IN TE DOMINE SPERAVI.
South German about 1600.
Blade l. 104.4 cm. Hilt l. 21 cm.
M.182–1921.

10
Sword, the gilt-steel hilt
encrusted with silver.
Saxon (Dresden) about 1550.
The blade is inscribed MIGUEL
CANTERO and EN SOLO DIO
CONFIO.
Blade l. 91.5 cm. Hilt l. 18 cm.
M.11–1955.

11
Rapier, the hilt of gilt bronze
cast and chased with strapwork
and masks, the blade pierced,
inscribed with letters and the
name FEDERICO PICININO.
Saxon (Dresden) about 1600.
This hilt may be by the
Dresden master Israel Schuech
who worked for the Elector
Christian I.
Blade l. 97 cm. Hilt l. 21.3 cm.
M.73–1949.

12
Rapier, the steel hilt gilt,
engraved and chiselled.
Saxon (Dresden) about 1590.
The hilt is by Othmar Wetter,
swordsmith to the Elector of
Saxony at Dresden, and was
probably made for the Elector
Christian I.
Blade l. 92.1 cm. Hilt l. 19.5
cm.
M.74–1949.

13
Rapier, the hilt of chiselled and
blued steel.
Saxon (Dresden) about 1590.
On the blade are the Spanish
royal arms and the badges of
Ferdinand and Isabella of Spain.
The blade is inscribed
SEBASTIANES HERNANDOS.
Blade l. 97.3 cm. Hilt l. 20 cm.
1748–1947.

14 and 15
Rapier and dagger, the hilts of
blued and chiselled steel.
Saxon (Dresden) about 1590.
Rapier: Blade l. 98 cm. Hilt l.
19 cm.
Dagger: Blade l. 26.2 cm. Hilt
l. 12 cm.
M.34 & a–1948.

were also often filled with plates. From the 17th century these plates often featured as two large shells which in turn developed into a cup-guard. Fashionable especially in Spain and Italy the cup-hilt rapier continued to be used in Spain until the very end of the 18th century when the rest of Europe had adopted the small-sword. A clumsy version of the cup-hilt rapier known as a *bilbo* was still being used as a military weapon in Spain during the Napoleonic Wars. In England the cup-hilt was made up of a series of linked bars, the base filled with twin shells. Cup-hilt rapiers seem, from the evidence of their appearance in English portraits, to have been used up to the 1630s. Rapier hilts were so variously constructed during the 17th century that it is very difficult to isolate national characteristics. A peculiarity of English hilts from the late 16th to the middle of the 17th century however is the use of a large globular pommel and counter-curved quillons, folded close to the other parts of the hilt, which gives them a very ungainly appearance. The Thirty Years War (1618–48) had an important influence by spreading different styles of hilt throughout northern Europe; the Flemish rapiers known as 'Pappenheimers', used widely on the Continent, were carried by officers of many northern European nations, throughout this period.

16
Rapier, the steel hilt encrusted with silver and inlaid along the edges with silver chain, the blade inscribed FRANSISCO RUIZ EN TOLEDO.
French, about 1590.
Blade l. 96 cm. Hilt l. 15 cm.
M.73–1953.

17
Rapier, the steel hilt encrusted and inlaid with silver and chiselled, the blade inscribed SAHAGUM.
Flemish, about 1630–40.
Blade l. 89.5 cm. Hilt l. 16.3 cm.
Timperley Collection, Castle Museum, York.

18

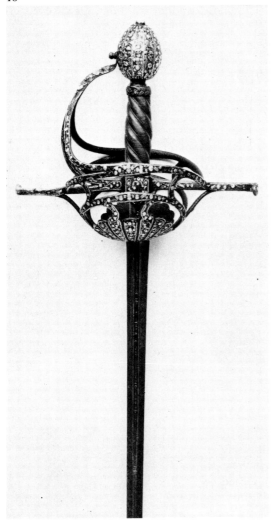

19

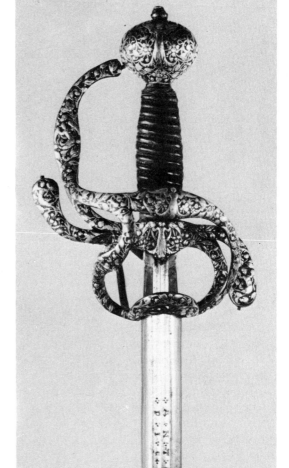

18
Rapier, the hilt encrusted with
silver, the blade inscribed
TOMAS AIALA EN TOLEDO
ANNO 1550.
English, about 1630.
Blade l. 96 cm. Hilt l. 19.7 cm.
M.2753–1931.

19
Rapier, the hilt of steel
encrusted with silver, the blade
inscribed ANTONIO PICINIO.
English, about 1600.
Blade l. 104.5 cm. Hilt l. 20
cm.
M.55–1947.

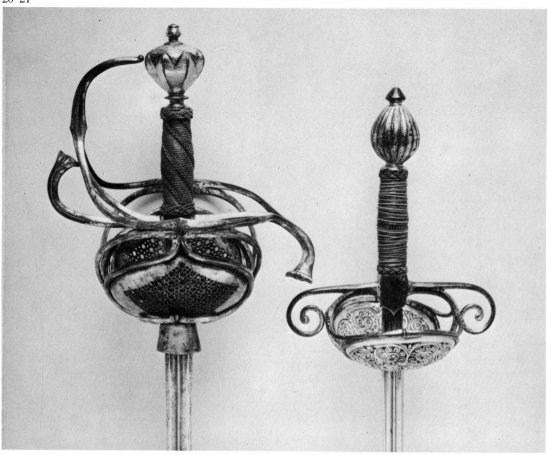

Because styles became international it is extremely difficult to attribute the decoration or manufacture of a rapier hilt to individual craftsmen or countries. Important sources for any attributions are the surviving designs for sword-hilts, produced by a number of artists from the 16th century onwards. Well-known artists like Hans Holbein are known to have designed swords and daggers, but the majority of designs that still exist are the work of goldsmiths. These include Erasmus Hornick (*ob.* 1583) who worked in Nuremberg around 1560, Pierre Woeriot who worked in Lyons at about the same time, and Antoine Jacquard of Poitiers who worked during the first half of the 17th century. Jacquard actually made swords and guns, and his designs show more practicality than some of his fellow artists. It is rare to find close links between an actual sword and a design. The work of French designer Etienne Delaune in the latter half of the 16th century is an exception to this. His designs were used by the school of craftsmen established at the Munich court in the 17th century. Three masters in particular produced some beautiful

20
Rapier, the steel hilt plated with silver and decorated with punched work.
Flemish, about 1630.
This type of rapier known as a 'Pappenheimer' was widely used during the Thirty Years War (1618–48).
Blade l. 112 cm. Hilt l. 22 cm.
M.50–1946.

21
Rapier, the hilt of gilt steel fitted with plates of pierced and gilt brass.
German, about 1650.
Blade l. 101 cm. Hilt l. 21.3 cm.
M.2–1950.

22 and 23
Rapier and dagger, the steel
hilts pierced and chiselled.
Italian (Naples) about 1650.
The hilts are signed by the
Neapolitan craftsman Antonio
di Cilenta.
Rapier: Blade l. 98 cm. Hilt
l.18 cm.
Dagger: Blade l. 47.7 cm. Hilt
l. 13 cm.
M.56–1947 & M.124–1921.

hilts, the ornament based on the designs of Delaune. These were
Emanuel Sadeler (*ob.* 1610), Daniel Sadeler (*ob.* 1632) and Caspar
Späat (*ob.* 1691). Another important school was established at
the Saxon court at Dresden in the late 16th century. Othmar
Wetter (*ob.* 1598), an artist of this school, specialized in delicately
chiselled steel hilts. The signature of another Dresden maker
Israel Schuech appears together with the date 1606 on a magnificent swept-hilt rapier of gilt bronze set with stones, formerly
in the Electoral Armoury at Dresden. The contents of this
armoury were absorbed into the collection of the Dresden His-
torical Museum. This collection is of paramount importance to
the historian of the sword, not only because of the magnificent
state of preservation of the swords but also on account of the
careful inventories that were kept from the 16th century. Also
working in Germany, but at a later date, was a Nuremberg
craftsman Gottfried Leygebe (1630–83), appointed 'coin-die
cutter' to the Elector of Brandenburg in 1668. This artist's
signature appears on the underside of the pommel on a light
rapier which bears decoration chiselled in iron, and depicting
the 'Labours of Hercules'; he is known to have made statuettes
in this intractable material.

24
Rapier, the hilt of cast silver, the blade inscribed MEFECIT SALINGEN.
English, about 1640.
Blade l. 82 cm. Hilt l. 15.5 cm.
M.2724–1931.

25
Rapier, the hilt of chiselled steel, the base of the pommel signed GOTFRID LEIGEBE.
German, about 1670.
Gottfried Leygebe was appointed 'Coin-die cutter' to the Elector of Brandenburg in 1668. He specialized in the art of chiselling iron, and produced not only sword-hilts, but also statuettes in iron.
Blade l. 91 cm. Hilt l. 15 cm.
M.59-1947

26
Rapier, the hilt of agate mounted in silver-gilt, the blade etched with mottoes.
French, about 1650.
Blade l. 71.5 cm. Hilt l. 13.8 cm.
M.14-1964

27
Rapier, the steel hilt chiselled with the 'Labours of Hercules'.
French, about 1655.
Blade l. 75.2 cm. Hilt l. 16.2 cm.
M.659–1910.

The Small-Sword

In the second quarter of the 17th century new fencing techniques developed in France. These techniques demanded the use of the point rather than the edge of the sword, and also depended upon great speed in attack and defence. A new kind of light rapier was developed to satisfy the demands of the new style which was known as a small-sword, in England. The classic small-sword combined elements from a number of different swords. Included in its ancestors are the long rapiers with guards consisting of two large shells, straight quillons and small arms of the hilt and the very light rapiers with short blades and simple cross hilts, known as scarf-swords, since they were worn on a sash at the waist or over the shoulder. Some very fragile and elegant examples of this latter form have been preserved with hilts of crystal or onyx. These early precursors of the classic small-sword are shown on a number of French and Dutch portraits and on engravings dating from the period c. 1630–60.

28
Rapier, the hilt of cast and chased silver, the blade inscribed BISCOTTO – the name of swordsmiths working in Villa Basilica near Lucca, Italy. Dutch, about 1650.
This sword or one identical to it, is shown on a painting of 1651 by Jan Albertsz. The painting depicts members of the Town Militia of Hoorn, Holland. The sword is worn by Sergeant Josyas Wybo.
Blade l. 76 cm. Hilt l. 14.8 cm.
M.111–1953.

29
Small-sword, the hilt of enamelled gold.
Dutch (Amsterdam) about 1670, the blade inscribed FRANCISCO (RU) IZ EN TOLETO.
Maker's mark of Joannes Kalkoen of Amsterdam.
Blade l. 68.8 cm. Hilt l. 15 cm.
M.60–1947.

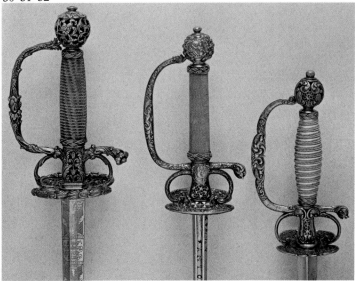

30
Small-sword, the hilt of
pierced and chiselled steel, the
blade engraved with mottoes.
Italian (Brescia) about 1690.
The blade probably dates from
the early 18th century.
Blade l. 90 cm. Hilt l. 17.3 cm.
M.17–1956.

31
Small-sword, the hilt of
pierced and chiselled steel, the
blade inscribed ANTONIO RUIS.
Italian (Brescia) about 1690.
Blade l. 82 cm. Hilt l. 16.7 cm.
M.71–1947.

32
Small-sword, the hilt of
pierced and chiselled steel, the
blade 18th century.
Italian (Brescia) about 1690.
Blade l. 74 cm. Hilt l. 16.8 cm.
M.2728–1931.

When the sword was held correctly the fingers were passed
through two small rings underneath the guard known as the
arms of the hilt. This enabled the fencer to manoeuvre the point
more easily. In the early development stages of this form of hilt
these arms were made large enough to accommodate the fingers.
However by the 1670s this practice was abandoned and the arms
of the hilt were gradually reduced. Small-swords with knuckle-
bows are shown in paintings as early as the mid-17th century,
but it was not until the end of the century that these became
universally adopted. Once the classic form of the small-sword
had developed, its basic shape underwent only minor changes.
In general, hilts with large arms of the hilt, and shells with
prominent rims, can be dated to the 17th century, while early
pommels on small-swords are ovoidal or of flattened horizontal
section. As well as the small-swords with knuckle-guards or
guards formed of twin shells, a type of sword having a very
simple form of hilt with a loop guard was also worn. The loop
guard consisted of a knuckle-bow and single quillon with an
outward curving bar springing from the central part of the
knuckle-bow to rejoin the guard at the quillon. Hilts of this
form appear as early as the 1640s and were popular throughout
the 18th century.

In the first part of the 18th century the small-sword underwent some changes. The curve of the knuckle-bow became
gentler and the rims of the shells flatter. Pommels were pear-
shaped and globular. As early as the 1720s the shell-guards of
certain English silver-hilted small-swords were linked by small
bars. By about 1760 the division between the two shells had
disappeared, the guard now consisting of one oval plate. From

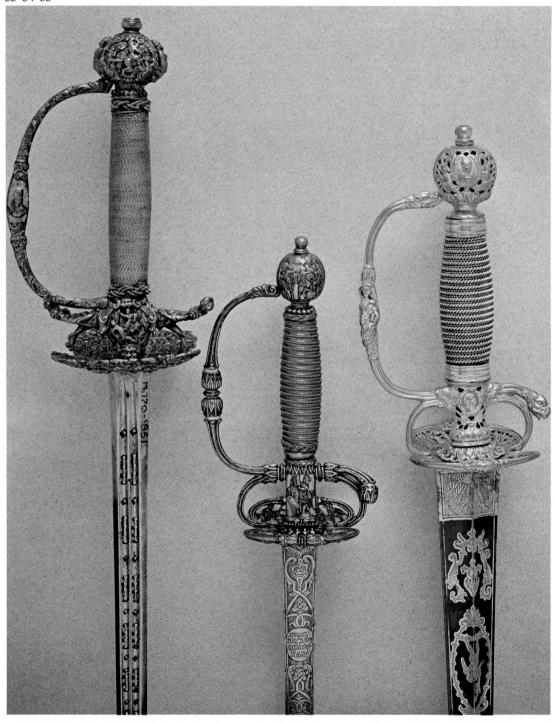

33
Rapier, the hilt of steel
chiselled, pierced and gilt.
French, about 1660.
The knuckle-bow has been
added in about 1740, to bring
the hilt up to the current
fashion.
Blade l. 92.5 cm. Hilt l. 17.8
cm.
M.170–1951.

34
Small-sword, the hilt of
chiselled steel, gilt and inlaid
with gold, the blade etched
with mottoes and
representations of the twelve
apostles.
French, about 1690.
Blade l. 75.3 cm. Hilt l. 16 cm.
M.2725–1931.

35
Small-sword, the hilt of cast
and gilt bronze, the blade
inscribed 'A DEUX SAISONS'.
French, about 1700.
Blade l. 78.8 cm. Hilt l. 17.4
cm.
1715–1888.

the middle of the 18th century, a guard in the form of a heart became fashionable for military swords, where it survived until the 1830s. In the late 18th century a pommel in the shape of a classical urn was introduced, reflecting the influence of Neo-Classicism. By this time the arms of the hilt had become very small upward curving bars close to the guard. By the early 19th century the guard often consisted of a single downward-turned shell, the arms of the hilt being abandoned altogether. Hilts of this form, with a very stylized urn-shaped pommel, became standard on swords made as part of formal court dress, and are still produced today for the same purpose.

Because the small-sword was worn principally as an adjunct to civilian dress, its decorative qualities were quite as important as its functional qualities. It has been justifiably observed that many swords are really masculine jewellery. The substantial shell-guards and other elements of the small-sword hilt provided opportunities for lavish decoration. A few 17th century small-swords with gold hilts have been preserved and some are decorated with enamels. It is recorded that hilts of gold designed by J. A. Meissonnier (1683–1750) were made as presents for the wedding of Louis XV in 1725. A small number of hilts has survived, which are clearly the work of craftsmen used to producing the elegant gold snuff-boxes so fashionable with the rich in the 18th century. Like the boxes, these hilts show every refinement of decoration, including the use of different coloured alloys of gold for decorative effect. Gold-hilted swords were often presented as rewards for gallantry, or for special services by grateful merchants. The gold presentation swords, made in the Neo-Classical taste in England towards the end of the 18th century and adorned with enamels, are probably the best known examples of this type of small-sword.

A large number of small-swords with silver hilts has survived, particularly from the 18th century. According to the evidence of inventories and newspaper advertisements for lost or stolen swords, silver was apparently also widely employed for making hilts during the 17th century but there are comparatively few surviving examples that can be dated before the 1670s. It seems clear from contemporary sources that styles of hilt changed quite quickly, and that old-fashioned silver hilts were often 'traded-in' for their melt value when a new hilt was acquired. Silver hilts are of importance to the chronological development of the small-sword because very many of them bear a full set of hallmarks including a date letter, and hilts of steel and brass can then be dated by a comparison of styles.

The majority of small-swords that have survived have hilts of steel. It is a measure of the skill of the hilt maker that he was able to produce such a variety of designs with such an intractable material. Some steel hilts are so finely worked that they can

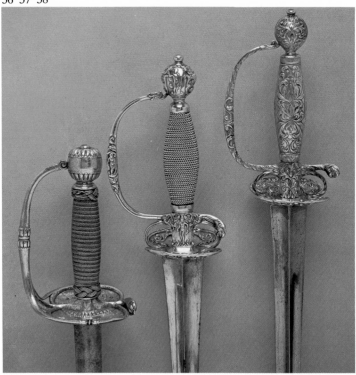

36
Small-sword, the silver hilt cast
and engraved, the blade etched
with mottoes.
English, London hallmarks for
1676–7.
Maker's mark WB.
Blade l. 78.2 cm. Hilt l. 13.8
cm.
M.153–1937.

37
Small-sword, hilt of cast and
chased silver.
English, about 1720.
Maker's mark IR.
Blade l. 81.5 cm. Hilt l. 16.0
cm.

38
Small-sword, the hilt of cast
and chased silver, matted with
a punch.
English, about 1725.
Blade l. 80.2 cm. Hilt l. 15 cm
Hammersmith Public Library.

39
Small-sword, the hilt of cast
and gilt silver.
French, Paris hallmarks for
1725–6.
Blade l. 81 cm. Hilt l. 14.5 cm.
1730–1888.

40
Small-sword, the silver hilt cast
and chased.
French, Paris hallmarks for
1744–5.
Blade l. 78.3 cm. Hilt l. 16.6
cm.
1718–1888.

41
Small-sword, the hilt of cast
silver.
French, Paris hallmarks for
1771–2.
Blade l. 75 cm. Hilt l. 17 cm.
1727–1888.

42
Designs for jewellery and a
small-sword hilt by David
Baumann.
German, about 1695.
The hilt was intended to be set
with precious stones.
E.1072–1908.

only have been made by craftsmen trained as medallists. At least one, Franz Matzenkopf of Salzburg (1705–76), is known to have decorated small-swords, for examples bearing his signature are preserved in Vienna and Turin. For hilts of good quality, chiselling, inlaid work and piercing were especially used. The surface was chiselled away to leave the design in low relief; the ground was then sometimes worked over with a matting punch and gilded. It should be remembered that very few steel hilts are preserved in their original condition, as the highly polished surface quickly oxydized in damp conditions. Frequent and drastic cleaning soon removed the subtleties of punched work, engraving and gilding. The few chiselled hilts that have survived in virtually pristine condition look almost garish: the relief ornament in mirror-bright steel contrasts sharply with the dull matted surface of the gilding. Inlaid work in gold and silver was frequently employed, particularly in the first quarter of the 18th century. The sword-cutlers of Tula in Russia, working in the 18th century, not only produced fine chiselled work in steel, usually with a deep gold ground, but also used a characteristic form of gold inlay. Large areas of the hilt were left plain and oxydized to a magnificent midnight blue; very delicately chiselled gold and silver flowers were then let into the surface at

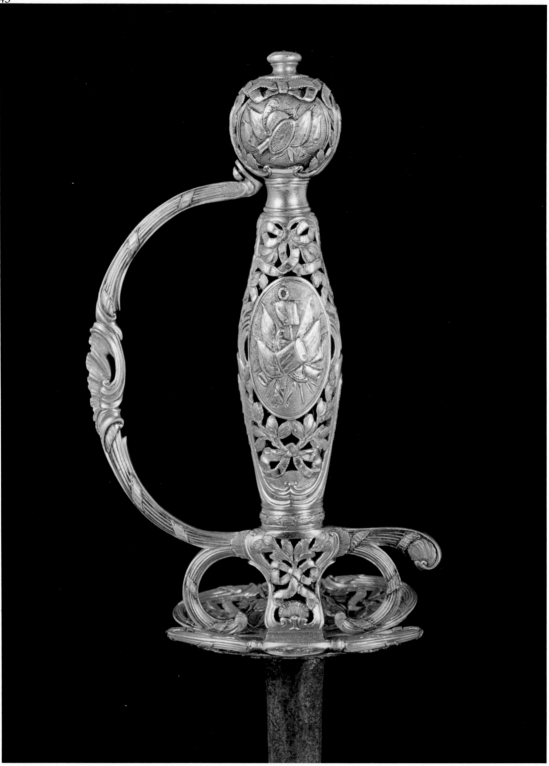

43
Small-sword, the hilt of three-coloured gold, pierced, chased and matted.
Swiss, about 1760.
The hilt is unmarked.
Blade l. 78.5 cm. Hilt l. 14.2 cm.
M.40–1973.

44
Small-sword, the hilt of chiselled and gilt steel, inlaid with gold, the blade inscribed FOUASSE MD FOURBISSEUR AU ROY DE LA CHINE SUR LE PONT ST MICHEL A PARIS.
French, about 1770–80.
Blade l. 80.2 cm. Hilt l. 17 cm.
1716–1888.

45
Small-sword, the chiselled steel hilt blued and gilt.
French or German, about 1770.
Blade l. 74.8 cm. Hilt l. 16.5 cm.
1738–1888

46
Small-sword, the hilt of steel, chiselled and gilt, set with a gold plaque bearing the cypher of Gustavus III, King of Sweden (1746–92).
Swedish, about 1770.
The blade bears the arms of Charles Manners Duke of Rutland (1754–87). This sword was probably a gift from the king.
Blade l. 86.2 cm. Hilt l. 16.3 cm.
M.193–1928.

44 45 46

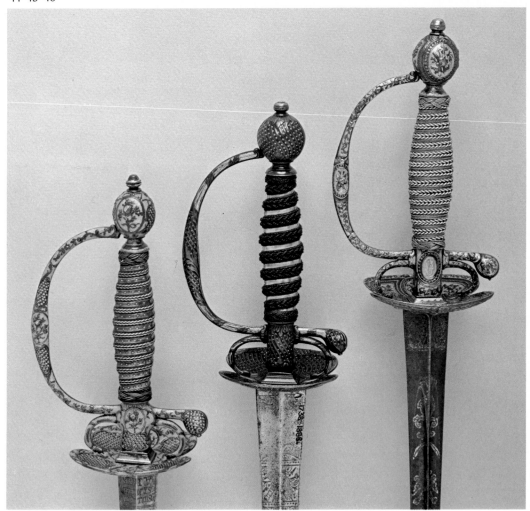

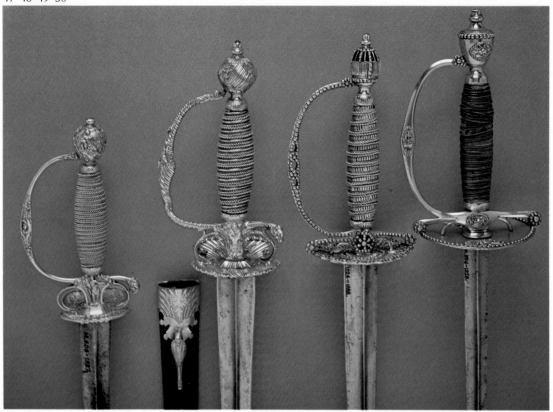

intervals. This decorative treatment had the advantage that the fragile elements of the hilt, such as the knuckle-bow and quillons, were not weakened by chiselling and piercing. Some very fine pierced hilts were produced in Italy during the 17th century, almost certainly in Brescia. In the finest examples large areas of the shell are left unpierced so that it still protects the hand, while the pommel and quillon block are pierced in the manner of fine lace work. Some excellent pierced hilts were made in England in the 1760s, the shells being pierced in a rayed design. Matthew Boulton and John Fothergill, in their factory established in the 1770s at Soho, Birmingham, specialized in the manufacture of burnished steel hilts set with facetted studs. Some of these hilts are mounted with Wedgwood cameos. A number of English steel hilts in a similar style, but decorated with gold inlay, survive; some of these are signed by Gray of Bond Street, which suggests that Boulton did not have a monopoly in the manufacture of this type of sword.

A few small-sword hilts of cast bronze are known, usually gilded and almost certainly cast in a mould and 'worked-up' with a chisel afterwards. Brass was also used for hilts produced by the casting process; such hilts were almost invariably gilded

47
Small-sword, the hilt of silver-gilt, cast, chased and matted with a punch.
English, about 1720.
Blade l. 70.7 cm. Hilt l. 14.7 cm.
M.606–1927.

48
Small-sword, the hilt of cast and chiselled silver.
English, about 1750.
Maker's mark IR, the scabbard chape inscribed HERVETT TEMPLE BAR.
Blade l. 81.8 cm. Hilt l. 16.3 cm.
M.140–1978.

49
Small-sword, the hilt of pierced and facetted silver.
English, London hallmarks for 1776–7.
Blade l. 81.5 cm. Hilt l. 16.3 cm.
1724–1888.

50
Small-sword, the hilt of silver-gilt.
English, London hallmark for 1783–4.
Maker's mark of William Kinman.
Blade l. 82.7 cm. Hilt l. 16.5 cm.
M.956–1928.

51
Designs for the hilts of small-swords to be executed in gold.
French, about 1725.
By J. A. Meissonier (1693–1750).
E.228A–1893.

or silvered, though few traces of these surface coatings now remain. Mother of pearl, tortoiseshell, beadwork and porcelain were employed in the manufacture of small-swords during the 18th century – particularly on the Continent. A taste for the exotic was reflected in the use of chinoiserie design in the early part of the 18th century, especially on silver small-swords. An interesting group of hilts was made in Japan for the Dutch market. These hilts are made from *shakudo*, the copper and gold alloy widely used in Japan for sword-guards. The workshop making these hilts seems to have been in operation from about 1700 until nearly the middle of the 18th century, for, as well as the usual small-sword hilts with twin shells, hilts with heart-shaped guards dateable to about 1750 are also found.

One group of hilts decorated in a markedly northern Indian style is known. These hilts are of blued steel and most are of conventional small-sword form; the decoration is a delicate gold

52 53 54

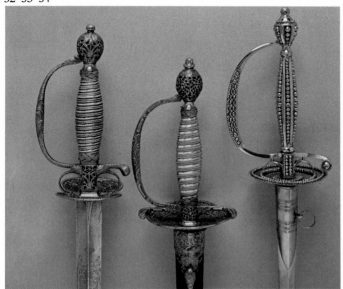

55 56 57

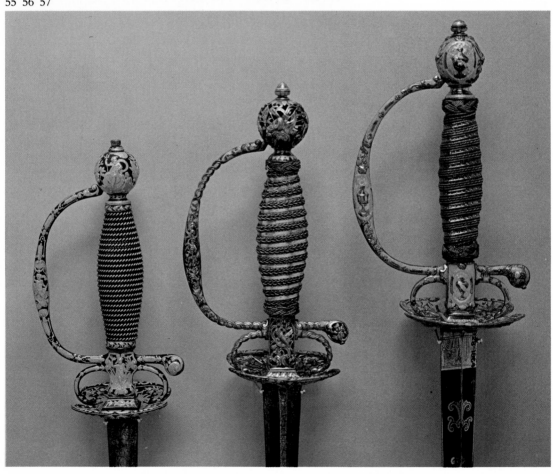

28

52
Small-sword, the hilt of
chiselled and pierced steel.
English, about 1760.
Blade l. 87.2 cm. Hilt l. 17.2
cm.
1720–1888.

53
Small-sword, the hilt of
chiselled and pierced steel, the
scabbard chape inscribed
STEVENS TEMPLE GATE.
English, about 1770.
Blade l. 83.2 cm. Hilt l. 16.7
cm.
M.192–1928.

54
Small-sword, the hilt of
burnished steel, set with steel
beads.
English, about 1775.
Blade l. 85.6 cm. Hilt l. 17.2
cm.
771–1889.

55
Small-sword, the hilt of steel
blued and overlaid with designs
in chased gold.
French, about 1730.
Blade l. 77 cm. Hilt l. 15.5 cm.
1717–1888.

56
Small-sword, the hilt of steel
pierced and chiselled, the
ground of matted gold.
French, about 1760.
Blade l. 97.2 cm. Hilt l. 16.8
cm.
M.72–1947.

57
Small-sword, the hilt of
chiselled steel, the ground gilt
and matted with a punch.
French, about 1780.
The hilt and blade are
exceptionally well preserved.
Blade l. 82 cm. Hilt l. 17 cm.
928–1864.

58
Sabre, the hilt of blued steel
inlaid with gold.
Northern Indian for the
European market, about 1770.
Blade l. 80.5 cm. Hilt l. 15 cm.
M.12 & a–1971.

59
Small-sword, the hilt of blued
steel inlaid with gold.
Northern Indian for the
European market, about 1760.
Blade l. 83.3 cm. Hilt l. 17 cm.
1723–1888.

inlay in a variety of Eastern designs. Eccentricities of construction, such as the form of the pommel, grip and shell indicate that the hilts were native copies of European swords or alternatively taken from European designs. Plain European hilts were also sent to India to be decorated. The majority of those hilts decorated in India date from the last quarter of the 18th century.

Some small-swords were made especially for children and exhibit every ornamental refinement found on their larger counterparts. Small-swords with twin-shell guards and loop guards survive, though the former are far more common. They seem to have been especially popular in the late 17th and early 18th centuries, judging from the numbers dating from this period which survive. These swords are usually fitted with blades cut down from full-length swords and thus have rather unhappy proportions, but examples exist with the blade trimmed down properly so as to make pleasing miniatures.

The Basket-Hilt

The origins of the basket-hilt, which has a network of bars and plates that entirely surrounds the hand, are not at present known. Primitive forms of basket-hilt are to be found on some

60
Small-sword, the hilt of
shakudo an alloy of copper and
gold.
Japanese, for the Dutch market,
about 1740.
Blade l. 79.3 cm. Hilt l. 15 cm.
M.277–1960.

61
Small-sword, the hilt of
shakudo, the blade inscribed
JEAN HOSSE MR ZWAARDFEGER
A AMSTERDAM.
Japanese, for the Dutch market,
about 1740.
Blade l. 79.5 cm. Hilt l. 15 cm.
1736–1888.

62
Hanger, hilt of *shakudo*, the
blade etched and gilt.
Japanese, for the Dutch market,
about 1700.
Blade l. 64.7 cm. Hilt l. 16.5
cm.
M.63–1950.

63
Hanger, the hilt of cast and
chased silver.
Japanese, for the Dutch market,
about 1690.
Blade l. 65.3 cm. Hilt l. 13.3
cm.
Grosvenor Museum, Chester.

64
Broadsword, the hilt of pierced
steel, the blade inscribed VIVAT
and PRO DEO FIDE ET PATRIA.
Scottish (Glasgow) about 1730.
The hilt is signed T. GEMMIL
ARMORER (*sic*).
Blade l. 89.2 cm. Hilt l. 15 cm.
M.83–1930.

65
Broadsword, the hilt of pierced
steel.
Scottish (Stirling) about 1730.
Fitted with the original lining
of buff leather lined with silk.
Blade l. 84 cm. Hilt l. 15.5 cm.
M.607–1927.

64
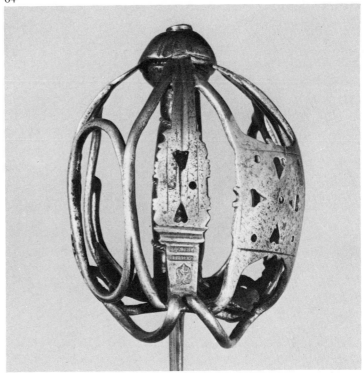

65

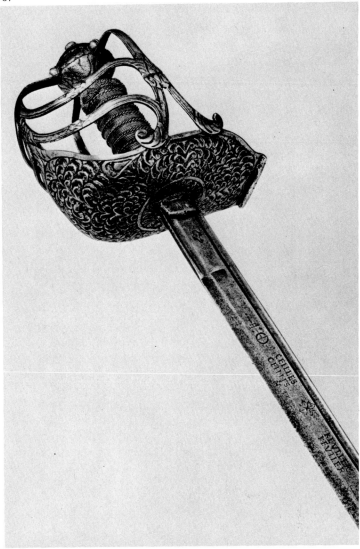

66
Broadsword, the guard of steel,
the pommel of cast brass,
plated with silver.
English, about 1635.
Probably made in the sword
factory at Hounslow.
Blade l. 77 cm. Hilt l. 14 cm.
Private Collection.

67
Basket-hilted sword, the hilt of
chiselled steel.
English, about 1640.
The blade inscribed CEILLES
KEULLER and SOLINGEN.
Blade l. 92 cm. Hilt l. 6.5 cm.
Private Collection.

German and Scandinavian swords of the second quarter of the
16th century. A developed form was certainly in use in England
by the second quarter of the century and was probably introduced to Scotland at about the same time. This type of hilt has
always been associated with Scotland, and perhaps the finest
Scottish examples were produced in the first half of the 18th
century. Makers such as Thomas Gemmill, the Simpsons of
Glasgow and Walter Allan of Stirling excelled in the production
of sturdy hilts decorated in a distinctive manner. With the Dis-
arming Acts and the introduction of mass-production methods
after 1745, the basket-hilt became stereotyped, although some
fine cut-steel basket-hilts were produced towards the end of the
18th century.

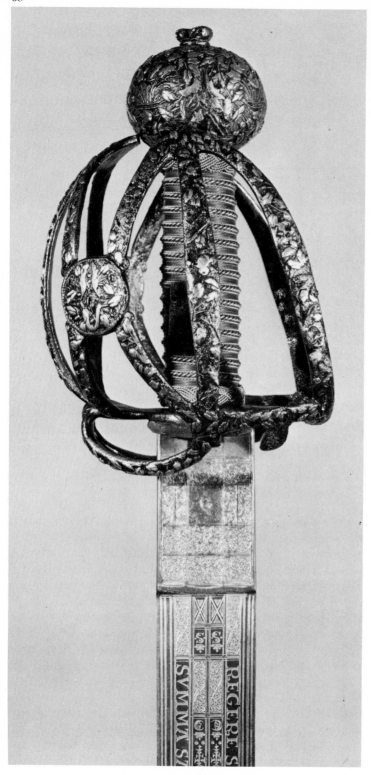

68
Basket-hilted broadsword, the
steel hilt encrusted with silver.
English, about 1600.
The blade is one of a group
engraved with the arms of
James I, supplied by Clemens
Horn of Solingen (1580–1630).
Blade l. 82.5 cm. Hilt l. 17.5
cm.
M.54–1957 & 472–1936.

69
Basket-hilted sword, the steel
hilt russetted, parcel-gilt and
inlaid with gold.
English, about 1660.
The blade which dates from
about 1640 is inscribed ME
FECIT HVNSLO.
The basket is pierced in the
design of an unidentified family
crest.
Blade l. 81 cm. Hilt l. 16.5 cm.
M. 439–1936.

70
Basket-hilted sword, the hilt of
chiselled steel.
English, about 1680.
The blade which dates from
about 1640 is inscribed ME
FECIT HOUNSLOE.
Blade l. 71.3 cm. Hilt l. 14.5
cm.
M.4–1956.

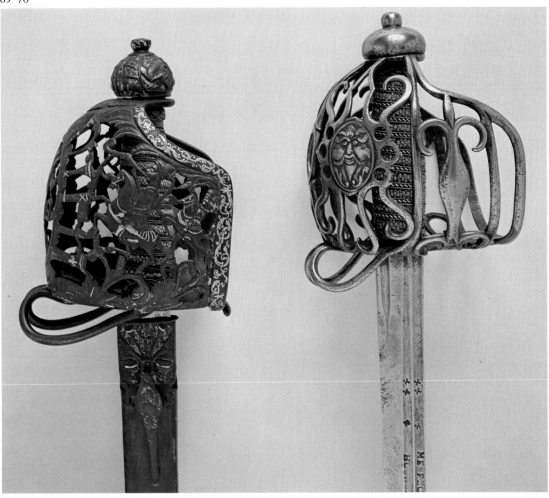

In England during the Civil War a type of basket-hilt known to collectors as a mortuary hilt was fashionable. The term 'mortuary' refers to the fact that many of the hilts are decorated with chiselled heads thought to commemorate Charles I. Very few of the chiselled heads actually resemble the king however, and it is clear that they are simply decorative motifs. These basket-hilts were carried by both Parliamentary and Royalist forces during the Civil War. They almost certainly derive from the hangers (literally a sword that hung from the belt) with large shell guards made in England in the 1630s.

The Hunting Sword

From the middle of the 17th century another type of sword was often carried by civilians – the *couteau de chasse* or hunting sword. Some of the the earliest hunting swords were specifically de-signed for killing boars, since to kill a boar on foot armed only

Hanger, the steel hilt inlaid with silver, the wooden grip set with engraved panels of mother of pearl and staghorn (one of the shells forming the guard is missing).
English (Hounslow), the blade inscribed IOHAN KINNDT HOUNSLOE 1634.
Blade l. 69.5 cm. Hilt 13.5 cm.
M.610–1937.

72
Hunting sword, the steel hilt inlaid with silver.
English, about 1640, the blade inscribed, 1551, with the Orb and Cross of Solingen.
Blade l. 69.5 cm. Hilt l. 17.6 cm.
M.2788–1931.

with a sword was seen as a great test of courage. However, the length of these weapons, about 1.5 metres, meant that they could not conveniently be carried, particularly when mounted. Most huntsmen preferred a short sword or hanger – a combination of the curved sword and a peasant knife. Their guards vary in construction but usually consist of a knuckle-bow combined with short quillons. One of the most interesting English examples, now at Windsor Castle, is that made for Henry VIII by Diego de Çaias in about 1545. This is fitted with a short curved blade, and into its scabbard is fitted a short by-knife. The scabbards of hunting swords were often fitted with pockets on the outside to take a variety of knives, bodkins and sharpening steels. Owing to the improvement in firearms, the hunting sword lost its role as the principal weapon of the hunt and became much more a weapon to be carried for everyday protection, its short blade making it very convenient for travelling.

Because the hunting sword was principally a civilian weapon, and was worn like the small-sword as an adjunct to civilian dress it quickly became an article of luxury and demanded the attentions of the goldsmith rather than the sword cutler. Hunting swords were often fitted with silver mounts, or, less commonly, were fitted with hilts entirely made from precious

73

Hunting sword, the hilt of cast, cast, pierced and engraved silver, the blade with the mark of the WUNDES family of bladesmiths.
English, about 1670.
Maker's mark a crowned letter.
Blade l. 47.7 cm. Hilt l. 12.6 cm.
937–1864.

74

Hunting sword, hilt of buck-horn mounted in silver, the mounts engraved with the owner's initials IF.
English, about 1670.
Maker's mark WS.
Blade l. 50 cm. Hilt l. 14.4 cm.
1776–1939.

75

Hunting sword, hilt of staghorn mounted in silver.
English, London hallmarks for 1702–3.
Blade l. 49.5 cm. Hilt l. 14 cm.
M.152–1922.

76

Hunting sword, the horn grip mounted in cast and chased silver.
English, about 1730.
Maker's mark IR.
The serrated edge enabled the sword to be used as a saw.
Blade l. 54.6 cm. Hilt l. 13.2 cm.
M.156–1922.

77

Hunting sword, the horn grip mounted in cast and chased silver.
English, London hallmarks for 1739–40.
Maker's mark PM.
Blade l. 56 cm. Hilt l. 13.2 cm.
M.157–1922.

78

Hunting sword, the grip of agate mounted in cast and chased silver.
English, London hallmarks for 1739–40.
Blade l. 55.2 cm. Hilt l. 13.1 cm.
M.155–1922.

73 74 75

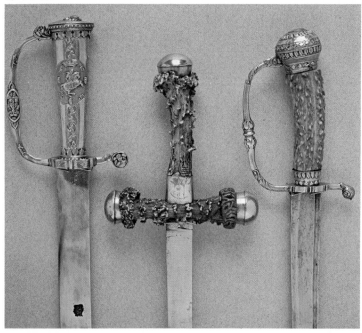

76 77 78

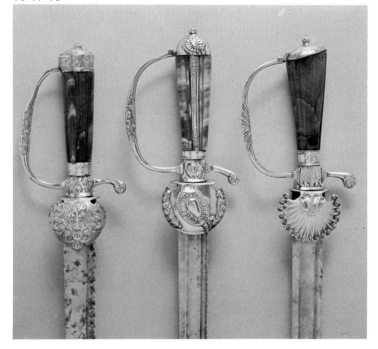

metals. Fragile materials such as agate, or even porcelain, are found on 18th century hilts. Some hunting swords were constructed from tortoiseshell decorated with gold piqué work. As with small-swords, some of the German and French design books illustrate the hilts of hunting swords. Certain hunting swords, particularly during the 18th century, have flintlock pistols mounted on the blade, close to the guard. It has been suggested that they were used to give the *coup de grâce* to a wounded animal. A few very decorative examples, mostly of German or eastern European origin, have recesses in the blade into which are set watches or portrait miniatures. These are far too fragile to have ever been used, and were presumably made simply as curiosities. In skilled hands the hunting sword could be a deadly weapon: for example, in Paris in about 1750 the celebrated fencing master Domenico Angelo, armed only with a hunting sword, was able to beat off an unexpected attack by an assailant with a small-sword. During the 19th century some very decorative hunting swords were produced for exhibition purposes, with elaborate and clumsy hilts in the Gothic style, and in Germany at the present day several cutlers in Solingen are producing hunting swords which bear at least some resemblance to the austere and practical productions of their predecessors.

79
Hunting sword, the hilt and scabbard of silver, parcel-gilt.
French, about 1850.
Made by the firm of Marrel Frères of Paris, this was shown at the Great Exhibition of 1851.
Blade l. 45 cm. Hilt l. 15 cm.
159–1851.

80
Design for the hilt of a hunting sword by J. L. Wuest.
German (Augsburg) about 1730.
13625.3.

Blades

It is impossible for several reasons to produce a chronology of the sword based on styles of blade. Old blades were often cut down and re-hilted years after they were made; blades broke and had to be replaced. Moreover, swords have suffered, as have so many other arms, from what one writer on the subject has described as the 'vicissitudes of private ownership'. The lamentable custom of replacing a genuine but plain blade, which has been with its particular hilt for many years, with a more decorative blade taken from some other sword so as to produce a pleasing but composite sword, cannot be too strongly condemned. This practice, which has been carried on for at least a hundred years, has meant that only a comparatively small percentage of the swords in private and public collections are fitted with their original blade.

The manufacture of blades on a large scale for international consumption was concentrated in a few centres. The most prolific was undoubtedly Solingen in the German Rhineland, which dominated the swordsmiths' trade from the Middle Ages until comparatively recently. Cologne was also celebrated for its blades. In Italy blades were made in Pavia, Venice, Milan, and particularly Brescia. In Spain the cities of Valencia and Toledo were paramount. In England a sword factory was established at Hounslow in the 1620s, staffed by Solingen craftsmen, and the end of the 17th century saw the establishment of a factory at Shotley Bridge in Northumberland, which survived until 1832. Birmingham and Sheffield became important centres for the manufacture of sword blades in the 18th century. The Solingen trade especially seems to have unashamedly copied both the marks and names of other makers. Any inscription on a blade, therefore, should be interpreted with the greatest caution. Large numbers of blades are to be found bearing the names of well-known Toledo makers, but with a distinctly Germanic spelling. The blades of many Scottish swords are inscribed with the name Andria Ferrara in a variety of spellings. Although a maker of this name is said to have worked in Belluno, Italy, in the 16th century, many of these blades are incised with the Running Wolf mark of the Solingen and Passau bladesmiths, and it appears that most are German. Scottish blades were well-known enough for one Solingen cutler to mention, in a letter of 1628, *Grosse Schotten* blades (i.e. broad Scottish blades) as one of the products he offered for sale. Old and valued blades were often retained long after their original hilts had perished. It is still possible to find a regulation Scottish hilt dating from the end of the 19th century fitted with a fine mid-17th century German blade, although the Running Wolf mark of Solingen may be almost buried in a mass of etched thistles and regimental badges.

81
Small-sword, the gold hilt set with enamel plaques.
English, London hallmarks for 1813–14 with the maker's mark of John Ray and James Montague.
Presented by the City of London to Lieut.-General Rowland Hill for services at the battle of Vittoria in 1813.
Blade l. 83 cm. Hilt l. 18.5 cm.
M.50–1963.

82
Small-sword, the gold hilt decorated with *champlevé* enamel.
English, London hallmarks for 1781–2 with the maker's mark of James Morriset.
This sword was presented to Lieut.-Col. James Hartley by the Honourable East India Company for saving the army from annihilation during the 1st Mahratta War (1775–82).
Blade l. 83 cm. Hilt l. 17 cm.
M.39–1960.

83
Small-sword, the hilt of silver-gilt decorated with enamel.
English, London hallmarks for 1798–9 with the maker's mark of James Morriset.
Presented to Lieutenant Francis Douglas of HMS Repulse by the Committee of Merchants of London for services during the mutiny at the Nore in 1797.
Blade l. 86 cm. Hilt l. 18.2 cm.
274–1869.

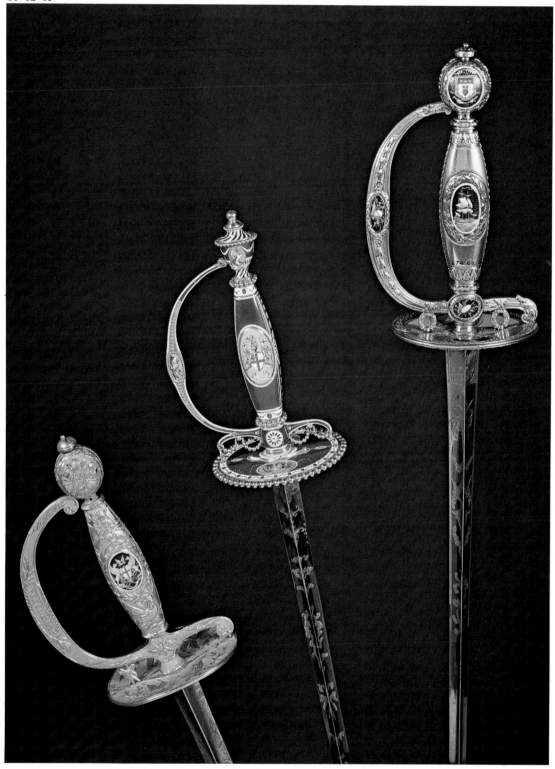

Blades were forged by hand in the same manner as hand-made cutlery is produced today. The tang – the extension of the blade that passes through the grip – was nearly always welded on to the blade, and many blades made before the 19th century show clear traces of the welded joint a short way down the blade. The process of forging a sword blade has changed very little, although modern sword-cutlers use machine-driven hammers. Bars of steel of suitable quality are heated and forged to the correct shape. They are then 'tempered' to reduce any stresses in the structure of the metal. This consists of placing the blade in a bath of molten lead which gives an even temperature along its entire length and then quenching the hot blade in a bath of oil. The blade is then ground and polished. This last process is carried out in almost exactly the same manner as was used in the 17th century; the craftsman lies flat, holding the blade against a revolving grindstone.

Small-swords are found fitted with a variety of blades. In the 17th century, a flat, fairly broad blade with the Running Wolf mark of the Passau or Solingen cutlers was often used. A blade with a broad forte, tapering very suddenly, was developed in about 1680. Most of the weight of the sword was therefore in the hilt allowing the point to be moved very rapidly. Blades of this form were known as Colichemarde or Königsmark blades, and were said to have been named after the Swedish soldier of fortune and duellist Count Königsmark (1665–94), who particularly favoured them. The fencing master Sir William Hope, writing in 1685, advocated the use of a 'narrow three cornered blade' as by far the lightest; a substantial number of small-swords are fitted with blades of this type. However it is clear from such sources as the Diderot Encyclopaedia of about 1755 that other forms were mounted in small-sword hilts. Blades of flattened diamond section and hexagonal section, and simple double-edged flat blades with long fullers (grooves sometimes thought to allow the blood to run but more probably cut simply to save weight) are all illustrated in the Encyclopaedia article on sword-cutlers. Very few have survived with their original decoration intact. It is clear that many were originally gilded and blued, and often blades show traces of engraved or etched ornament on the forte with designs of strapwork, trophies, naïve sketches of oriental figures, or scrolls. One group, probably made in Solingen, is decorated with the twelve apostles down the length of the blade, each with his name underneath. At the beginning of the 19th century, a method of decorating blades by acid etching became fashionable. The surface of the background was also treated with acid to give a frosted effect which contrasted with the bright steel of the elements of the main design. This method of decorating blades is still in use and certain old-established English sword-cutlers have design books

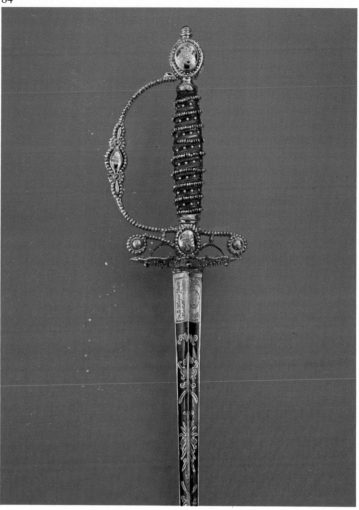

84
Small-sword, the hilt of cut
steel decorated with gold.
English (London) about 1780,
the blade inscribed DE LE
MARQUE DES MOUCHETTE A
SOLINGEN.
The scabbard chape is inscribed
GRAY, BOND ST.
Blade l. 82.5 cm. Hilt l. 16 cm.
M.40 & a–1971.

for blade decoration going back well into the last century.

The most popular swords for cavalry during the 18th century
were fitted with a single-edged curved blade. Swords with
curved blades were used in Switzerland and Germany from the
16th century. The campaigns against the Turks in Europe towards the end of the 17th century seem to have led to the
adoption by most European armies of the single-edge curved
blades carried by their Turkish adversaries, and curved blades
fitted with a variety of hilts were carried by most armies until
this century.

Scabbards
A disappointingly small number of swords of all periods survive
with their original scabbards. The best proof that a blade is
original to the hilt is the presence of a scabbard with mounts

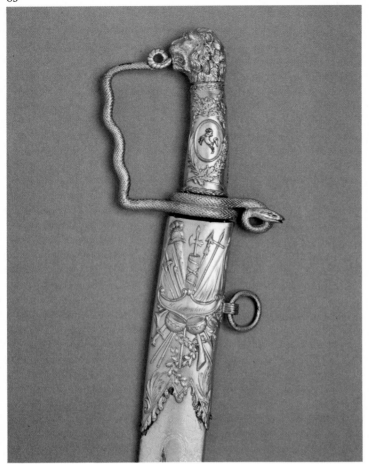 

decorated *en suite* with the hilt. A very clear description of scabbard manufacture is given in the Diderot Encyclopaedia of 1755. Thin veneers of beechwood cut into strips were fitted around the blade, sewn leather or linen put around the wooden strips and then a final outer covering of sewn leather or vellum was glued on. Metal mounts or chapes were fitted at both ends and a locket around the centre with a ring by which the scabbard could be suspended from the belt. Sometimes the mount at the top was omitted, and a hook slotted into the top of the scabbard. The top mount of the scabbard often bears the name of the vendor of the sword together with his address and is thus an important document for the historian of the sword. However broken and fragile, the original scabbard should always be retained.

Mass Production
When large numbers of men had to be provided with swords, it was both easier and more economical if all the swords were

85

Presentation sabre, the hilt of silver, cast, chased and gilt, the Turkish blade inlaid with gold. English London hallmarks for 1804–5, Maker's mark BL. This sword belonged to Charles, Earl Whitworth (1752–1825) as Colonel Commandant of the Holmsdale Infantry.
Blade l. 76.5 cm. Hilt l. 13.8 cm.
1606–1871.

86

Sword, the mounts of silver gilt, the scabbard of mother of pearl.
French (Versailles) 1802–3.
This is one of a group of swords made for members of the Consulate Government by Nicholas Noël Boutet.
Blade l. 75.5 cm. Hilt l. 15 cm.
486–1870.

87

Rapier, the hilt of silver-gilt.
Spanish or Portuguese, about 1750.
Blade l. 81 cm. Hilt l. 15.5 cm.
M.4–1968.

88

Sword of a *Commissaire de guerre*, the hilt of cast silver, the blade inscribed IS & C.
French, Paris hallmarks for 1809–19
Blade l. 97.3 cm. Hilt l. 18.2 cm.
Joicey Museum, Newcastle.

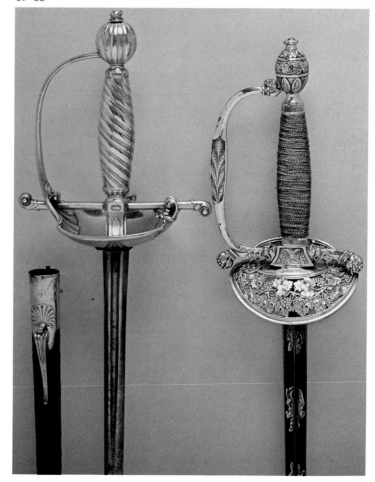

of a similar pattern. Some degree of uniformity in equipment prevailed in the armies of the Middle Ages, but it was not until the middle of the 17th century, when standing armies became common in Europe, that swords were made to a design covered by Government regulations. These designs varied from country to country, but in general they all share the characteristics of simplicity of construction and cheapness of manufacture. It is clear that certain patterns of hilt, such as the so-called 'Walloon' type, were used all over Europe during the second half of the 17th century. These hilts are characterized by a stout double-shell guard of pierced steel and a short double-edged blade. Brass was widely used for regulation hilts from the 17th century because of its cheapness and also because it could be easily cast in a mould. The rough and worn ornament to be found on many brass hilts indicates that the moulds must have been re-used many times. Officers usually provided their own swords, and in consequence these were of much better quality. Some of the swords made by cutlers for English officers during the Napoleonic Wars, especially those with hilts of pierced and chiselled steel, are particularly remarkable.

Forgeries

During the 19th century the demand for highly decorated arms led more than one iron-worker to produce forgeries of the lavish hilts of the 16th century. One of the cleverest forgers of the swordsmith's art was the Dresden locksmith Anton Konrad who died in 1938. Working in close association with a well-established Berlin antique dealer named Kahlert, Konrad had access to the fine 16th century swords in the Dresden Museum, and was able to make excellent copies of them. His great skill combined with the frequent use of original blades allowed many of his swords to be sold as genuine. Kahlert took advantage of the fact that at the time the Dresden Museum was selling off genuine items from its collections, and gave the museum as the provenance for many of the swords made by Konrad. The latter made many different kinds of sword, but his copies of rapiers and daggers in the Saxon style of the late 16th century are probably his most successful efforts. His work is often betrayed by discrepancies between the excellent condition of the hilts and the worn and pitted blades, which were often genuine; no amount of cleaning or scouring could remove all the traces of age on the blades. It is often said that Konrad's hilts are too large, but comparison with authentic pieces shows that the proportions of a Konrad piece usually reflect those of the genuine article. Most of the major collections of swords include at least one piece by this master, and his best work bears comparison with many period pieces.

89

89
Sword, the hilt of chiselled steel, the blade stamped with pseudo makers' marks and incised with letters.
German, in the Spanish style of about 1570 but almost certainly made by Anton Konrad of Dresden in about 1920. The blade has been sprayed with acid to give the appearance of corrosion.
Blade l. 99.2 cms. Hilt l. 24.2 cms.
M.44–1947.

Further Reading

A comprehensive study of the sword in Europe has yet to be written, and although the bibliography of the sword is extensive, there are many aspects of the subject which are not discussed. Some of the best studies on individual swords are buried in obscure periodicals.

For the study of the medieval sword, useful books are:

Boccia, L. G. B. and Coelho, E. T., *Armi Bianchi Italiani*, Milan, 1975.
Hoffmeyer, Ada Bruhn, *Middlalderens Tveaggede Svaerd*, Tojhusmuseet, Copenhagen, 1954 (with English summary.)
Oakeshott, R. E., *The Sword in the Age of Chivalry*, London, 1964.

Some of the most accurate and current information is contained in the catalogues of private and public collections. Those listed below are well illustrated and have accurate texts:

Blair, C., The James A. de Rothschild Collection at Waddesdon Manor, *Arms, Armour and Base Metalwork*, Fribourg, 1975.
Dufty, A. R., *European Swords and Daggers in the Tower of London*, London, 1974.
Haenel, E., *Kostbare Waffen aus der Dresdner Rustkammer*, Leipzig, 1923.
Mann, Sir James, *European Arms and Armour*, (Wallace Collection Catalogues) London, 1962.
Schobel, J., *Princely Arms and Armour*, London, 1975.

The collections in Dresden and Vienna are particularly important as they contain virtually the finest examples of the swordsmith's art preserved in almost perfect condition.

General books which contain good sections on European swords are:

Blair, C., *European and American Arms*, London, 1962.
Hayward, J. F., *Swords and Daggers*, (Victoria and Albert Museum) London, 1963.
Laking, Sir Guy F., *A Record of European Armour and Arms through Seven Centuries*, 5 vols., London, 1920-2.
Seitz, H., *Blankwaffen*, 2 vols., Brunswick, 1964.

For hunting swords the best account is given in:

Blackmore, H. L., *Hunting Weapons*, London, 1971.

The important collection of hunting swords in the Metropolitan Museum, New York, is discussed in:

Dean, Bashford, *European Court Swords and Hunting Swords*, New York, 1929.

There are several books which deal with particular nationalities and types of sword. For Scottish swords the best books are:

Wallace, J., *Scottish Swords and Dirks*, London, 1970.
Whitelaw, C. F., *Scottish Arms Makers*, London, 1977. (This contains important studies on basket-hilt makers.)

For British 'Regulation' swords:

Robson, B., *Swords of the British Army*, London, 1975.

For Russian swords:

Mavrodin, V., *Fine Arms from Tula*, Leningrad, 1977.

For naval swords:

Annis, P. G. W., *Naval Swords*, London, 1970.
May, W. E. and Annis, P. G. W., *Swords for Sea Service*, London, 1970.

American swords have quite an extensive literature. The best sources are:

Neumann, G. G. C., *Swords and Blades of the American Revolution*, Newton Abbot, 1973. (This also has a large number of illustrations of European swords.)
Peterson, H. L., *The American Sword*, New Hope Penn., 1954.

Because hilts are very rarely signed, there are very few studies on individual makers. One of the most important was Gottfried Leygebe. The only comprehensive study on this matter is:

Bruhn, Ada, *Der Schwertfeger Gottfried Leygebe*, Copenhagen, 1945. (Some of Bruhn's attributions are not accepted by modern authorities.)

Iron chisellers' work is discussed in:

Stocklein, H., *Meister des Eisenschittes*, Esslingen am N., 1922.

One of the ways of dating a sword-hilt is by its appearance on a dated or dateable painting. The following is an excellent study of some Guild Portraits in Hoorn:

Sloot, R. B. F. Van Der and Kist, J. B., *Some Facts Concerning Sword Hilts at Hoorn around the Year 1650*, Leiden, 1971.

The small-sword has been the subject of a number of books because of its decorative qualities. The following works are the most important:

Aylward, J. D., *The Small-Sword in England*, New edition, London, 1960. (Many items from this author's collection were given to the V & A.)

Dean, Bashford, *Op. cit.*

Hayward, J. F., 'The Origin of Small-sword Ornament', 'Sources of Small-sword Ornament', *Apollo, xlviii* (1948) 33–5, 86–8, 103–4, 107–8; *xlix* (1949) 76–80.

Dr. J. F. Hayward has written other important studies on designs for sword-hilts, including the following:

'Mannerist Sword Hilt Designs', *Livrustkammaren*, viii (1958–60), 79–109.

Designs are also discussed in his: *Virtuoso Goldsmiths*, London, 1976.

Swordsmiths' marks are often illustrated in catalogues. However the only individual and reliable text on the subject is:

Weyersberg, A., *Solingen Schwertschmeide des 16 und 17 Jahrhunderts und ihre Erzeugnisse*, Solingen, 1926.

There are many journals and periodicals which publish articles on European swords. The list below is a selection of the most important; the *Journal of the Arms and Armour Society of London* publishes a comprehensive list of current titles with each issue. The journal *Waffen- und Kostumkunde* contains some of the most important studies on the subject and should be the sword historian's *vade mecum*.

Armes Anciennes, 2 vols., Geneva, 1953–9.

Armi Antichi, Bolletino dell'Accademia di S. Marciano, Turin (in progress).

Connoisseur, London (in progress).

Journal of the Arms and Armour Society, London (in progress).

Livrustkammaren. Journal of the Royal Armoury, Stockholm (in progress).

Svenska Vapenhistoriska Arsskrift. Journal of the Swedish Arms and Armour Society, Stockholm (in progress).

Vaabenhistoriske Aarboger. Journal of the Danish Arms and Armour Society, Copenhagen (in progress).

Zeitschrift für Historische Waffenkunde. Journal of the Verein für Historische Waffenkunde. 17 vols., Dresden and Berlin, 1897–1944. Continued from 1955 to 1959 as *Mitteilungen der Gesellschaft für Historische Kostum- und Waffenkunde*, Berlin, and from 1960 as *Waffen- und Kostumkunde* (Munich and Berlin) (in progress).